# rockschool®

# POPULAR MUSIC THEORY

# Workbook

**GRADE 1**

www.rockschool.co.uk

# Acknowledgements

Published by Rockschool Ltd. © 2015
Catalogue Number RSK011504
ISBN: 978-1-908920-70-6
16 January 2017 | Errata details can be found at *www.rslawards.com*

## Publishing
Written, compiled and edited by Simon Troup, Jennie Troup and Stuart Slater.
Internal design and layout by Simon and Jennie Troup, Digital Music Art.
Cover designed by Philip Millard, Philip Millard Design.
Additional proofing by Chris Bird, Owen Bailey, Nik Preston, Mike Stylianou, Joanna Taman and Mary Keene.

## Syllabus Consultants
Rachael Meech, Mike Stylianou, Joanna Taman and Anna Cook.

## Contributors
Prof. Joe Bennett, Simon Niblock, Jonathan Preiss, Stefan Redtenbacher, Philip Henderson and Martin Hibbert.

## Images & Illustrations
*pp.* 24 & 47 | © iStock.com/craftvision
*p.* 25 | © iStock.com/58shadows
*p.* 27 | © grmarc / Shutterstock.com
*p.* 27 | © mitay20 / Shutterstock.com
*p.* 48 | © GrashAlex / Shutterstock.com

## Printing
Printed and bound in the United Kingdom by Caligraving Ltd.

## Distribution
Exclusive Distributors: Music Sales Ltd.

## Contacting Rockschool
*www.rslawards.com*
Telephone: +44 (0)845 460 4747
Email: info@rslawards.com

# Table of Contents

**Introductions & Information**

*Page*

**Theory Exam Sections**

*Page*

**Sample Paper**

*Page*

**Additional Information**

*Page*

# Welcome to Rockschool Popular Music Theory – Grade 1

Rockschool publish two sets of books to help candidates prepare for theory examinations – the *Rockschool Popular Music Theory Guidebooks* and *Rockschool Popular Music Theory Workbooks.*

The guidebooks are a teaching resource for candidates to work through the material required for the Rockschool theory syllabus with the support of their teacher.

To complement the guidebooks, a set of workbooks provide a series of exercises and sample papers in which to practise the skills introduced in the guidebooks.

### Entering Rockschool Examinations

It's now easier than ever to enter a Rockschool examination. Simply go to *www.rockschool.co.uk/enter-online* to book your exam online today.

### Syllabus Content Overview

An overview of the syllabus content covered at this grade can be found at the back of this book. As this is a cumulative syllabus, you can download overviews for all grades from the Rockschool website at *www.rockschool.co.uk/theory* along with other theory syllabus related resources.

### Exam Format

The exam has four sections. These are:

- **Music Notation** (20%)
  In this section, all questions relate to music notation.

- **Popular Music Harmony** (25%)
  In this section, all questions relate to music harmony.

- **Band Knowledge** (25%)
  This section is in two parts, with each part covering a range of instruments:
  – **Part 1:** Identification
  – **Part 2:** Notation and Techniques

- **Band Analysis** (30%)
  In this section, the questions will include the identification of music notation, harmony and the stylistic characteristics of drums, guitar, bass, keys and vocals in a multi-instrumental context.

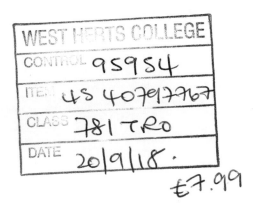

# SECTION 1 | MUSIC NOTATION

| SUMMARY | |
|---|---|
| SECTION *(Current section highlighted)* | MARKS |
| > **Music Notation** | **20 [20%]** |
| Popular Music Harmony | 25 [25%] |
| Band Knowledge | 25 [25%] |
| Band Analysis | 30 [30%] |

The *Music Notation* section of Rockschool Theory Examinations covers the following:

- 1.1    Pitch
- 1.2    Note length/rhythm
- 1.3    Dynamics, articulations and phrasing

You will be presented with a variety of exercises to hone your understanding and skills in these areas within the content specified for this grade.

## Content Overview

An overview of the syllabus content covered at this grade can be found at the back of this book. As this is a cumulative syllabus, you can download overviews for all grades from the Rockschool website at *www.rockschool.co.uk*.

# Section 1 | Music Notation

### Note lengths | Add barlines

1. Add barlines to the following stave, ensuring that there are the correct number of beats in each bar:

2. Add barlines to the following stave, ensuring that there are the correct number of beats in each bar:

3. Add barlines to the following stave, ensuring that there are the correct number of beats in each bar:

### Note lengths | Add time signatures

1. Add the correct time signature to the start of the following stave:

2. Add the correct time signature to the start of the following stave:

3. Add the correct time signature to the start of the following stave:

## Note lengths | Add missing notes

1. Add a note of the correct length above each question mark so that each bar matches the time signature:

2. Add a note of the correct length above each question mark so that each bar matches the time signature:

3. Add a note of the correct length above each question mark so that each bar matches the time signature:

## Note lengths | Beaming notes

1. Rewrite the music in bars 1 & 2 into bars 3 & 4, connecting the notes with beams where appropriate:

2. Rewrite the music in bars 1 & 2 into bars 3 & 4, connecting the notes with beams where appropriate:

3. Rewrite the music in bars 1 & 2 into bars 3 & 4, connecting the notes with beams where appropriate:

# Section 1 | Music Notation

**Note lengths | Equivalent notes and rests**

1. For every note there is a rest of the same length. Complete the following pairs by drawing the equivalent note or rest in the empty bars on the right:

2. For every note there is a rest of the same length. Complete the following pairs by drawing the equivalent note or rest in the empty bars on the right:

3. For every note there is a rest of the same length. Complete the following pairs by drawing the equivalent note or rest in the empty bars on the right:

**Note lengths | Adding together note and rest values**

1. Add together the value of the notes and rests on the left, then write a single note of the same total value on the right:

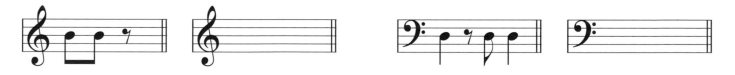

2. Add together the value of the notes and rests on the left, then write a single note of the same total value on the right:

3. Add together the value of the notes and rests on the left, then write a single note of the same total value on the right:

**Note names | Adding clefs**

1. Add the correct clef to the beginning of the stave below to make a major scale. Finally, tick the correct scale name in the box below the stave:

☐ C major    ☐ G major    ☐ F major

2. Add the correct clef to the beginning of the stave below to make a major scale. Finally, tick the correct scale name in the box below the stave:

☐ C major    ☐ G major    ☐ F major

3. Add the correct clef to the beginning of the stave below to make a major scale. Finally, tick the correct scale name in the box below the stave:

☐ C major    ☐ G major    ☐ F major

**Note names | Identifying chords**

1. In the example below there are three consecutive notes that form a G major chord. Put a circle around these three notes:

2. In the example below there are three consecutive notes that form an F major chord. Put a circle around these three notes:

3. In the example below there are three consecutive notes that form a C major chord. Put a circle around these three notes:

# Section 1 | Music Notation

## Accidentals | Sharps, flats and naturals

1. Compare the two bars on the right and identify which of the following statements is correct: *(Tick one box)*

☐ The note in bar 1 is higher than the note in bar 2.

☐ The note in bar 2 is higher than the note in bar 1.

☐ The notes in both bars are the same pitch.

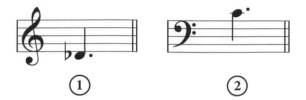

2. Compare the two bars on the right and identify which of the following statements is correct: *(Tick one box)*

☐ The note in bar 1 is higher than the note in bar 2.

☐ The note in bar 2 is higher than the note in bar 1.

☐ The notes in both bars are the same pitch.

3. Compare the two bars on the right and identify which of the following statements is correct: *(Tick one box)*

☐ The note in bar 1 is higher than the note in bar 2.

☐ The note in bar 2 is higher than the note in bar 1.

☐ The notes in both bars are the same pitch.

## Accidentals | Writing accidentals

1. Copy the four notes on the left into the empty bar on the right, rearranging the notes so that they are in order of pitch, from the lowest to the highest:

2. Copy the four notes on the left into the empty bar on the right, rearranging the notes so that they are in order of pitch, from the lowest to the highest:

**Repeats | Identifying repeat marks**

1. Examine the following four bars (which are written out in full and do not use repeat notation) then proceed to the next step:

The following three examples use repeat notation. When played, which example will produce the same melody as the four bars above? *(Tick one box)*

☐ Example 1    ☐ Example 2    ☐ Example 3

**Repeats | Using repeat marks**

1. Examine the following ten bars (which are written out in full and do not use repeat notation) then proceed to the next step:

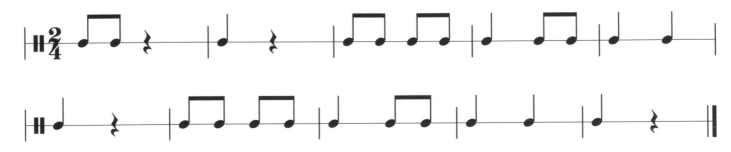

Rewrite the music above into the empty stave below, using repeat bars to enable you to fit the notes onto a single line:

# Section 1 | Music Notation

## Dynamics & Articulations | Identifying dynamics

1. Complete the blank spaces in the table below:

| SYMBOL | NAME OF SYMBOL | MEANING |
|---|---|---|
| < | Crescendo | Getting louder |
| *p* | | Quiet |
| > | Diminuendo | |
| | Forte | Loud |

## Dynamics & Articulations | Identifying articulations

1. Draw lines between the boxes to match the symbols (one of the left boxes) with their name (one of the centre boxes) and their meaning (one of the right boxes):

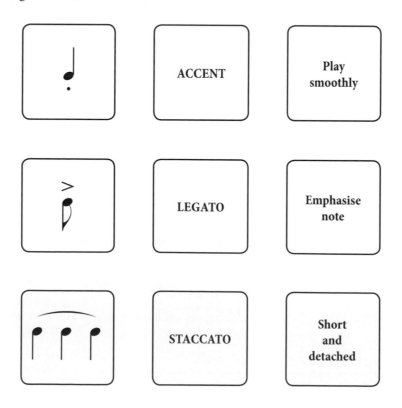

ACCENT — Play smoothly

LEGATO — Emphasise note

STACCATO — Short and detached

# SECTION 2 | POPULAR MUSIC HARMONY

| SUMMARY | |
| --- | --- |
| **SECTION** *(Current section highlighted)* | **MARKS** |
| Music Notation | 20 [20%] |
| > **Popular Music Harmony** | **25 [25%]** |
| Band Knowledge | 25 [25%] |
| Band Analysis | 30 [30%] |

The *Popular Music Harmony* section of Rockschool Theory Examinations covers the following:

- 2.1  Scales and related intervals
- 2.2  Simple triadic chords

You will be presented with a variety of exercises to hone your understanding and skills in these areas within the content specified for this grade.

### Content Overview
An overview of the syllabus content covered at this grade can be found at the back of this book. As this is a cumulative syllabus, you can download overviews for all grades from the Rockschool website at *www.rockschool.co.uk*.

# Section 2 | Popular Music Harmony

**Intervals | Identifying major seconds**

1. Tick the boxes of all of the following melodic intervals that are a major 2nd apart:

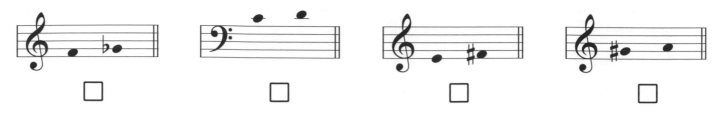

2. Add a note a major 2nd higher to the right of each of the following notes:

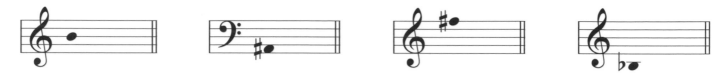

3. Add a note a major 2nd higher to the right of each of the following notes:

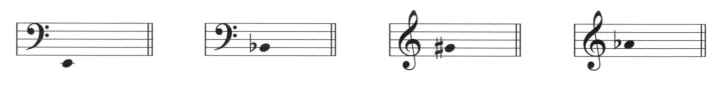

---

**Intervals | Identifying major thirds**

1. Tick the boxes of all of the following harmonic intervals that are a major 3rd apart:

2. Add a note a major 3rd higher to the right of each of the following notes:

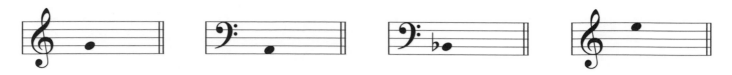

3. Add a note a major 3rd higher to the right of each of the following notes:

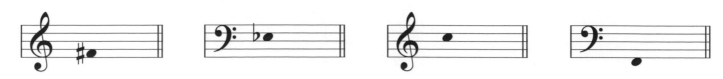

## Scales | Identifying scale intervals

1. Write 'T' in boxes between notes that are a **Tone** apart, and write 'S' in boxes between notes that are a **Semitone** apart:

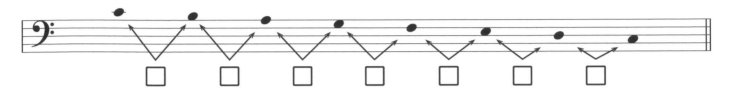

2. Write 'T' in boxes between notes that are a **Tone** apart, and write 'S' in boxes between notes that are a **Semitone** apart:

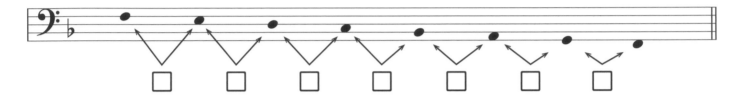

3. Write 'T' in boxes between notes that are a **Tone** apart, and write 'S' in boxes between notes that are a **Semitone** apart:

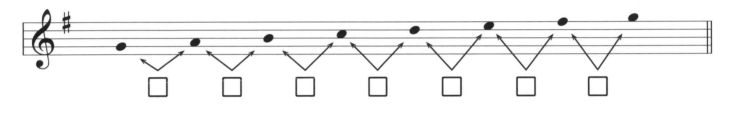

## Scales | Writing scales with accidentals

1. Using whole notes, write a one-octave *descending* scale of G major. Use accidentals instead of a key signature:

2. Using whole notes, write a one-octave *ascending* scale of F major. Use accidentals instead of a key signature:

3. Using whole notes, write a one-octave *ascending* scale of C major. Use accidentals instead of a key signature:

# Section 2 | Popular Music Harmony

**Scales | Writing scales with key signatures**

1. Using the key signature shown below, add the notes of a one-octave *ascending* major scale in whole notes:

2. Using the key signature shown below, add the notes of a one-octave *descending* major scale in whole notes:

3. Using the key signature shown below, add the notes of a one-octave *descending* major scale in whole notes:

4. Using whole notes, write a one-octave *ascending* scale of C major. Add the correct key signature if needed:

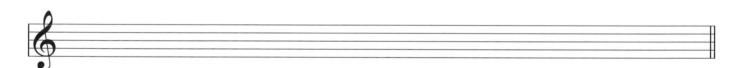

5. Using whole notes, write a one-octave *descending* scale of G major. Add the correct key signature if needed:

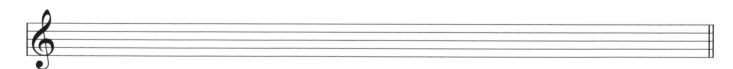

6. Using whole notes, write a one-octave *ascending* scale of F major. Add the correct key signature if needed:

## Scales | Add accidentals

1. This melody is in G major. Write out the melody again on the empty stave below. Use accidentals instead of a key signature:

2. This melody is in F major. Write out the melody again on the empty stave below. Use accidentals instead of a key signature:

3. This melody is in G major. Write out the melody again on the empty stave below. Use accidentals instead of a key signature:

4. This melody is in F major. Write out the melody again on the empty stave below. Use accidentals instead of a key signature:

# Section 2 | Popular Music Harmony

## Scales | Applying scale knowledge

1. Circle any notes that are **not** in the G major scale:

   G    A    B    C    D    E    F    G

2. Write out the letter names of the C major scale (with their accidentals if appropriate):

   *Your answer:* ...........................................................................................................................................

3. Write out the letter names of the G major scale (with their accidentals if appropriate):

   *Your answer:* ...........................................................................................................................................

4. Circle any notes that are **not** in the F major scale:

   C    D    E    F♯    G    A    B    C

5. Add any musical symbols that are necessary to correct this F major scale:

   F    G    A    B    C    D    E    F

6. Look at each note in turn, circling those that can be found in the G major scale:

   F♯    B    C    B♭    G♮    E    D    C♯    F    A    D♭    A♮    G    E♮

7. Briefly describe the function of a 'flat' sign:

   *Your answer:* ...........................................................................................................................................

   ...........................................................................................................................................................

8. Briefly describe the function of a 'natural' sign:

   *Your answer:* ...........................................................................................................................................

   ...........................................................................................................................................................

## Arpeggios | Identifying arpeggios

1. This is an *ascending* and *descending* F major arpeggio. Add the correct clef and key signature:

2. This is an *ascending* and *descending* C major arpeggio. Add the correct clef and key signature:

3. This is an *ascending* and *descending* G major arpeggio. Add the correct clef and key signature:

4. Using whole notes, write a one-octave *ascending* and *descending* arpeggio in the **major** key shown by the clef and key signature:

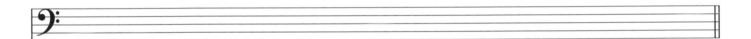

5. Using whole notes, write a one-octave *ascending* and *descending* arpeggio in the **major** key shown by the clef and key signature:

6. Using whole notes, write a one-octave *ascending* and *descending* arpeggio in the **major** key shown by the clef and key signature:

# Section 2 | Popular Music Harmony

**Chords | Writing correct chords**

1. Circle the major chord that shares its name with the key indicated by the key signature and clef. Finally, add the chord name on the line below the stave:

.................................................     .................................................

2. Circle the major chord that shares its name with the key indicated by the key signature and clef. Finally, add the chord name on the line below the stave:

.................................................     .................................................

3. Write the notes of an F major chord in the left stave and a C major chord in the right stave. Pay careful attention to the clef in each case. Finally, below each stave, write the names of the notes used in each chord:

     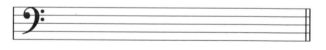

.................................................     .................................................

4. Write the notes of a G major chord in the left stave and a C major chord in the right stave. Pay careful attention to the clef in each case. Finally, below each stave, write the names of the notes used in each chord:

.................................................     .................................................

**Scales | Applying chord knowledge**

1. Circle the group of three notes that form a G major chord:

   G A B        G C D        G B E        G B D        G C E

2. Circle the group of three notes that form a C major chord:

   C F C        C E G        C D E        C F B        C E A

3. Circle the group of three notes that form an F major chord:

   F A B        F B E        F A C        F G A        F D E

4. Which major chord can be formed by rearranging the notes B, D and G?

   *Your answer:* ..................................................................................................................................

5. Tick the boxes of note groups that correctly form a major chord. Put crosses in the boxes of any groups that don't form major chords:

   ☐ G B D        ☐ F A C        ☐ C E A

6. Which three of the following musical terms are more frequently used when discussing chords? *(Tick three boxes)*

   ☐ Quarter

   ☐ Thirds

   ☐ Dot

   ☐ Major

   ☐ Time signature

   ☐ Minor

# Section 2 | Popular Music Harmony

### Chords | Applying chord knowledge

1. In the table below the top row is complete. Add the missing information in the following three rows to complete the table:

| MUSIC | CHORD NAME | NOTES |
|---|---|---|
| 𝄞 (chord) | C major | C   E   G |
| 𝄢 ♯ (chord) | G major | |
| 𝄢 (chord) | | |
| 𝄞 ♭ (chord) | | F   _   _ |

2. There are enough notes in the circles below to make a C major chord, an F major chord and a G major chord. Draw lines connecting the circles to create one of each chord, using each circle only once:

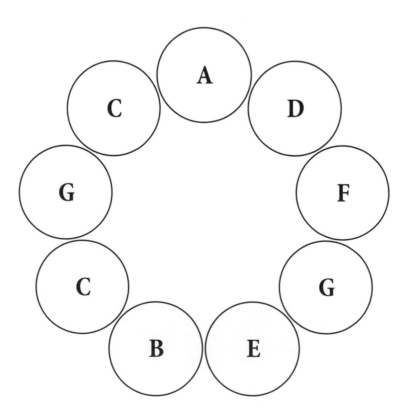

# Section 3 | Band Knowledge

| SUMMARY | |
| --- | --- |
| **SECTION** *(Current section highlighted)* | **MARKS** |
| Music Notation | 20 [20%] |
| Popular Music Harmony | 25 [25%] |
| > **Band Knowledge** | **25 [25%]** |
| Band Analysis | 30 [30%] |

The *Band Knowledge* section of Rockschool Theory Examinations covers the following:

- 3.1   Identify instrument parts and function
- 3.2   Identify instrument-specific notation
- 3.3   Identify instrumental techniques

You will be presented with a variety of exercises to hone your understanding and skills in these areas within the content specified for this grade.

## Content Overview

An overview of the syllabus content covered at this grade can be found at the back of this book. As this is a cumulative syllabus, you can download overviews for all grades from the Rockschool website at *www.rockschool.co.uk*.

# Section 3 | Band Knowledge

**Part 1 | Identification | Drums**

*The following five questions refer to the labelled image of a drum kit on the right:*

1. Which letter corresponds to the snare drum? *(Tick one box)*

   ☐ A  ☐ B  ☐ C  ☐ D  ☐ E

2. Which letter corresponds to the ride cymbal? *(Tick one box)*

   ☐ A  ☐ B  ☐ C  ☐ D  ☐ E

3. Which letter corresponds to the hi-hat? *(Tick one box)*

   ☐ A  ☐ B  ☐ C  ☐ D  ☐ E

4. Which letter corresponds to the bass drum? *(Tick one box)*

   ☐ A  ☐ B  ☐ C  ☐ D  ☐ E

5. Which letter corresponds to the crash cymbal? *(Tick one box)*

   ☐ A  ☐ B  ☐ C  ☐ D  ☐ E

----------------------------------------------------------------

*True or false:*

6. The ride cymbal has a foot pedal:  ☐ True  ☐ False

7. The snare drum is the largest drum in the drum kit:  ☐ True  ☐ False

8. The crash cymbal consists of two cymbals mounted one above the other:  ☐ True  ☐ False

----------------------------------------------------------------

9. Which type of cymbal is operated by a foot pedal? *(Tick one box)*

   ☐ Hi-hat  ☐ Ride  ☐ Crash

10. Which type of cymbal is usually placed on the drummer's right-hand side? *(Tick one box)*

    ☐ Hi-hat  ☐ Ride  ☐ Crash

11. Which type of cymbal is used for occasional accents, often at the end of phrases? *(Tick one box)*

    ☐ Hi-hat  ☐ Ride  ☐ Crash

**Part 1 | Identification | Guitar and Bass**

*The following three questions refer to the labelled image below:*

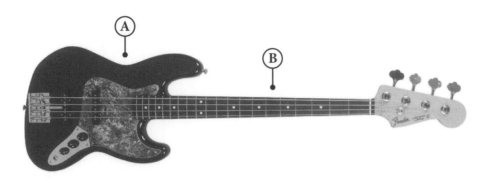

1.  What type of instrument is shown in the image above?

    *Your answer:* .........................................................................................................................

2.  What is the correct name for the part of the instrument that is labelled 'A'? *(Tick one box)*

    ☐ Foot   ☐ Body   ☐ Arm   ☐ Neck   ☐ Head

3.  What is the correct name for the part of the instrument that is labelled 'B'? *(Tick one box)*

    ☐ Foot   ☐ Body   ☐ Arm   ☐ Neck   ☐ Head

---

*True or false:*

4.  A guitar will usually have a longer neck than a bass guitar:   ☐ True   ☐ False

5.  All guitar bodies are shaped the same:   ☐ True   ☐ False

6.  Right-handed guitarists use their right hand on the neck:   ☐ True   ☐ False

---

7.  Each string on a guitar or bass guitar is equipped with a tuning peg (also known as a machine head) to change the pitch. How many tuning pegs would you expect to find on a guitar? *(Tick one box)*

    ☐ 1   ☐ 2   ☐ 3   ☐ 4   ☐ 5   ☐ 6   ☐ 7   ☐ 8

8.  How many strings would you expect to find in a packet of bass-guitar strings? *(Tick one box)*

    ☐ 1   ☐ 2   ☐ 3   ☐ 4   ☐ 5   ☐ 6   ☐ 7   ☐ 8

# Section 3 | Band Knowledge

**Part 1 | Identification | Keys**

1. An electronic keyboard is often supplied with an external box wired with an electrical plug and a connector to attach to the keyboard. It is used to supply the correct amount of electrical current to the keyboard. What is it called? *(Tick one box)*

   ☐ Solar cell ☐ Battery pack ☐ Power adaptor ☐ Fuse box

2. One of the white keys, found roughly in the middle of the keyboard, is commonly used as a reference point on the keyboard. What is this note called? *(Tick one box)*

   ☐ Top C ☐ Middle C ☐ Key of C ☐ CD

3. Is a black key longer than, shorter than, or the same length as a white key? *(Tick one box)*

   ☐ Longer ☐ Shorter ☐ Same length

4. Which of the following instruments is less likely to have an on/off button? *(Tick one box)*

   ☐ Electronic keyboard ☐ Piano

---

*True or false:*

5. The power adaptor is used to control the volume of the keyboard:  ☐ True ☐ False

6. There are more white keys than black keys on a keyboard:  ☐ True ☐ False

7. Black keys are organised into repeating groups of three then four keys:  ☐ True ☐ False

8. There is a black key between every white key on the keyboard:  ☐ True ☐ False

9. Another name for the 'on/off' button is the 'power button':  ☐ True ☐ False

---

10. Draw a line from each box on the left to a box on the right that contains the closest matching content:

| | |
|---|---|
| middle C | black key |
| on/off button | white key |
| power adaptor | switches keyboard on |
| F sharp | powers keyboard from power outlet |

## Part 1 | Identification | Vocals

*The following three questions refer to the labelled illustration on the right:*

1. Which letter points to the mouth? *(Tick one box)*

   ☐ A     ☐ B     ☐ C     ☐ D

2. Which letter points to the lungs? *(Tick one box)*

   ☐ A     ☐ B     ☐ C     ☐ D

3. Which letter points to the trachea? *(Tick one box)*

   ☐ A     ☐ B     ☐ C     ☐ D

--------------------------------------------------------------------------------

*Match the description with the correct part of the body:*

4. Also known as the oral cavity, this is the main cavity where the sound is mixed and finally released: *(Tick one box)*

   ☐ Mouth     ☐ Jaw     ☐ Trachea     ☐ Lungs

5. These organs allow you to breathe as well as sing. The air these organs expel is used by the singer to create sound: *(Tick one box)*

   ☐ Mouth     ☐ Jaw     ☐ Trachea     ☐ Lungs

6. This bone and its control muscles allow a singer to change the shape of the space in their oral cavity which helps form different sounds: *(Tick one box)*

   ☐ Mouth     ☐ Jaw     ☐ Trachea     ☐ Lungs

7. This is an important tube that allows air to pass down through the oral cavity and into the organs with which you breathe: *(Tick one box)*

   ☐ Mouth     ☐ Jaw     ☐ Trachea     ☐ Lungs

# Section 3 | Band Knowledge

## Part 2 | Notation & Techniques | Drums

*The following four questions relate to the one-bar extract of drum notation on the right:*

1. Which two voices play in the first beat of the bar?
   *(Tick two boxes)*

   ☐ Hi-hat      ☐ Bass drum      ☐ Snare

   ☐ Crash      ☐ Ride

2. Do the stems for the cymbals go up or down? *(Tick one box)*

   ☐ Up      ☐ Down

3. What does the 'o' symbol indicate? *(Tick one box)*

   ☐ Open hi-hat    ☐ Closed hi-hat    ☐ Accented crash

4. What does the '+' symbol indicate? *(Tick one box)*

   ☐ Open hi-hat    ☐ Closed hi-hat    ☐ Ride cymbal

---

*The following four questions relate to the one-bar extract of drum notation on the right:*

*True or false:*

5. The bass drum does not play on beat 2:

   ☐ True      ☐ False

6. The hi-hat is played throughout the bar:

   ☐ True      ☐ False

7. The crash cymbal is played on the first beat of the bar:

   ☐ True      ☐ False

8. The upper part consists of a crash cymbal followed by several ride cymbals:

   ☐ True      ☐ False

**Part 2 | Notation & Techniques | Drums**

*The following three tasks require you to add notation to the stave below:*

1. Add a hi-hat part to the two bars above in a constant eighth-note rhythm.

2. Add a symbol above the first eighth note of beats 1 and 3 of each bar to show that the hi-hat is played open.

3. Add a symbol above the second eighth note of beats 1 and 3 of each bar to show that the hi-hat should be closed.

- - - - - - - - - - - - - - - - - - - - - - - - - - - - - - - - - - - - - - - - - - - - - - - - - - - - - - - - - - - - - - - -

*The following task requires you to add notation to the stave below:*

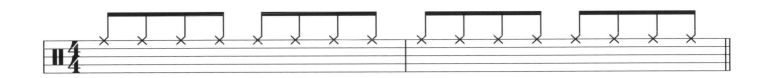

4. Add a part to the stave above as follows:

**Bar 1**
| Beat 1: | A quarter-note bass drum |
| Beat 2: | A quarter-note snare |
| Beat 3: | An eighth-note bass drum followed by another eighth-note bass drum |
| Beat 4: | A quarter-note snare |

**Bar 2**
| Beat 1: | A quarter-note bass drum |
| Beat 2: | An eighth-note snare followed by an eighth-note bass drum |
| Beat 3: | An eighth-note rest followed by an eighth-note bass drum |
| Beat 4: | A quarter-note snare |

# Section 3 | Band Knowledge

## Part 2 | Notation & Techniques | Guitar and Bass

*The following three questions relate to the one-bar extract of guitar notation on the right:*

1. Which technique should be used on the two notes in beat 2, indicated by a 'slur'? *(Tick one box)*

   ☐ Pull-off    ☐ Slide    ☐ Staccato

2. Which technique should be used on the two notes in beat 3, indicated by a straight line? *(Tick one box)*

   ☐ Strum    ☐ Pull-off    ☐ Slide

3. Which technique should be used on the last note of the bar, indicated by a dot above the note? *(Tick one box)*

   ☐ Slide    ☐ Staccato    ☐ Strum

---

*In this section you are asked to add notation symbols to the musical extract on the right:*

4. Add a slide symbol between the first two notes.

5. Add a symbol to show that a pull-off should be played between the third and fourth notes of the bar.

6. Add a staccato to the final note in the bar.

---

*True or false:*

7. A staccato note should be played as a short and detached note:

   ☐ True    ☐ False

8. A slide is played by strumming several strings at once:

   ☐ True    ☐ False

9. A pull-off is performed by sliding from one fret to another on the guitar or bass-guitar fingerboard:

   ☐ True    ☐ False

## Part 2 | Notation & Techniques | Keyboards

*The following four questions relate to the one-bar extract of piano/keyboard notation on the right:*

1.  Which hand plays staccato throughout? *(Tick one box)*

    ☐ Left      ☐ Right      ☐ Both

2.  Which hand plays legato notes throughout? *(Tick one box)*

    ☐ Left      ☐ Right      ☐ Both

3.  Which hand is playing the melody? *(Tick one box)*

    ☐ Left      ☐ Right      ☐ Both

4.  Which hand is playing the accompaniment? *(Tick one box)*

    ☐ Left      ☐ Right      ☐ Both

- - - - - - - - - - - - - - - - - - - - - - - - - - - - - - - - - - - - - - - - - - - - - - - - - - - - - -

*The following four questions relate to the one-bar extract of piano/keyboard notation on the right:*

*True or false:*

5.  The right hand plays the melody throughout:

    ☐ True      ☐ False

6.  The left hand plays the accompaniment:

    ☐ True      ☐ False

7.  The chords are all played staccato:

    ☐ True      ☐ False

8.  The melody is played legato throughout:

    ☐ True      ☐ False

# Section 3 | Band Knowledge

## Part 2 | Notation & Techniques | Vocals

*The following three questions relate to the one-bar extract of vocal notation on the right:*

1. How should the lyrics "I can" and "sky is" be sung?
   *(Tick one box)*

   ☐ With a slide    ☐ Staccato    ☐ Accented

*True or false:*

2. The notes in the first beat of the bar are legato:

   ☐ True    ☐ False

3. There is a portamento between the third and fourth notes of the bar:

   ☐ True    ☐ False

I can see the sky is clear

---

*The following question relates to the one-bar extract of vocal notation on the right:*

4. Is this music written for a female or male voice?
   *(Tick one box)*

   ☐ Female    ☐ Male

*The following two tasks require you to add notation to the one-bar extract of vocal notation on the right:*

5. Add staccato symbols to the final two notes of the bar.

6. Add a portamento symbol between the first two notes.

Some - where    in    the    dark - ness

---

*True or false:*

7. A bass singer has a lower pitch range than a tenor:    ☐ True    ☐ False

8. An alto singer is usually a male singer:    ☐ True    ☐ False

9. A soprano singer has a higher pitch range than an alto:    ☐ True    ☐ False

# SECTION 4 | BAND ANALYSIS

| SUMMARY | |
| --- | --- |
| **SECTION** (*Current section highlighted*) | **MARKS** |
| Music Notation | 20 [20%] |
| Popular Music Harmony | 25 [25%] |
| Band Knowledge | 25 [25%] |
| > **Band Analysis** | **30 [30%]** |

The *Band Analysis* section of Rockschool Theory Examinations covers the following:

- 4.1   Identify general music features
- 4.2   Accurately complete a score
- 4.3   Identify instrument-specific techniques

You will be presented with a variety of exercises to hone your understanding and skills in these areas within the content specified for this grade.

## Content Overview

An overview of the syllabus content covered at this grade can be found at the back of this book. As this is a cumulative syllabus, you can download overviews for all grades from the Rockschool website at *www.rockschool.co.uk*.

# Section 4 | Band Analysis

**Band Analysis | Example 1**

*The following 15 questions relate to the four-bar score below. Note that bar 2 has blank areas to be filled in as part of the tasks below:*

1.  What key is this piece in?


    *Your answer:* ..................................................................................................................................................

2.  In bar 2 of the vocal part (indicated by the asterisk) add a rest to complete the bar.

3.  In bar 2 of the guitar part, add chords that fit the chord symbols above the vocal line, in the following rhythm:

    Beat 1:   Quarter-note rest
    Beat 2:   Two eighth-note chords
    Beat 3:   Quarter-note rest
    Beat 4:   Quarter-note chord

4.  How many eighth notes would give the equivalent number of beats to the final rest in bar 4 of the guitar part? *(Tick one box)*

    ☐ 1    ☐ 2    ☐ 3    ☐ 4    ☐ 5    ☐ 6    ☐ 7    ☐ 8

5.  In bar 1, beat 1 of the piano part, add a musical symbol to indicate that the pianist should play loudly.

6.  In bar 4 of the piano part, add a decrescendo marking over beats 3 and 4.

7. Add a portamento symbol in the vocal part between the first two notes of bar 1.

8. Add symbols to all of the G major chords in the guitar part to show that they should be played short and detached.

9. In which bar or bars is the right hand of the piano part playing the same rhythm as the vocal line?

*Your answer:* ......................................................................................................................................

10. Which is the correct statement? *(Tick one box)*

☐ All three instrumental parts contain at least one rest.

☐ In beats 3 & 4 of bar 4, the vocal and guitar parts have a whole-note rest.

☐ In bar 1, the same rhythm is used in the left hand of the piano part and the guitar part.

☐ The guitar part is a four-bar melody.

☐ Both the vocal part and the right hand of the piano part start with a dotted quarter note in bar 3.

11. Identify the three notes that make up the chord in bar 4 of the guitar part:

*Your answer:* ......................................................................................................................................

12. In which bar does the left hand of the piano part play a note that is not part of the named chord? *(Tick one box)*

☐ Bar 1      ☐ Bar 2      ☐ Bar 3      ☐ Bar 4

13. Explain what information is provided by the tempo marking:

*Your answer:* ......................................................................................................................................

14. In which beat of bar 4 of the left hand of the piano part is there a melodic interval of a major 3rd ? *(Tick one box)*

☐ Beat 1      ☐ Beat 2      ☐ Beat 3      ☐ Beat 4

15. What type of barline is used at the end of bar 4?

*Your answer:* ......................................................................................................................................

# Section 4 | Band Analysis

**Band Analysis | Example 2**

*The following 15 questions relate to the four-bar score below. Note that bar 4 has blank areas to be filled in as part of the tasks below:*

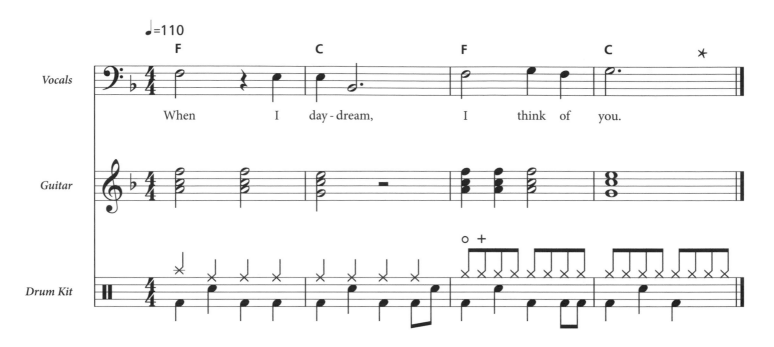

1. What is the tempo of this piece?

   *Your answer:* ...................................................................................................................................................

2. In bar 4 of the vocal part, indicated by the asterisk, add a rest to complete the bar.

3. In bar 4, beat 4 of the drum part, add notes in the following rhythm:

   *An eighth-note rest followed by an eighth-note snare drum.*

4. In bar 1, beat 1 of the vocal part, add a musical symbol to indicate that the vocalist should sing quietly.

5. In bar 4 of the drum part, add a musical symbol to indicate that the part should get gradually quieter during the first two beats of the bar.

6. Add a portamento symbol between the two notes in bar 2 of the vocal part.

7. Which part contains the longest note of the piece? *(Tick one box)*

   ☐ Vocal part ☐ Guitar part ☐ Drum part

8. Which is the correct statement? *(Tick one box)*

   ☐ The bass drum and snare play on beat 1 of bar 1.

   ☐ The bass drum and ride cymbal play on beat 1 of bar 1.

   ☐ The bass drum and crash cymbal play on beat 1 of bar 1.

   ☐ The bass drum and hi-hat play on beat 1 of bar 1.

9. Explain what the 'o' symbol means in bar 3 of the drum part:

   *Your answer:* ....................................................................................................................................

10. Explain what the '+' symbol means in bar 3 of the drum part:

    *Your answer:* ....................................................................................................................................

11. In the drum part, what is the upper drum voice played on beat 1 of bar 2?

    *Your answer:* ....................................................................................................................................

12. Name the melodic interval between the first two notes of bar 3 in the vocal part:

    *Your answer:* ....................................................................................................................................

13. Identify the three notes that make up the chord in bar 1 of the guitar part:

    *Your answer:* ....................................................................................................................................

14. How many eighth notes would give the equivalent number of beats to the dotted note in bar 4 of the vocal part?
    *(Tick one box)*

    ☐ 1   ☐ 2   ☐ 3   ☐ 4   ☐ 5   ☐ 6   ☐ 7   ☐ 8

15. Name the type of barline used at the end of the piece:

    *Your answer:* ....................................................................................................................................

# Section 4 | Band Analysis

**Band Analysis | Example 3**

*The following 15 questions relate to the four-bar score below. Note that bar 4 has blank areas to be filled in as part of the tasks below:*

1. What key is this piece in?

   *Your answer:* ........................................................................................................................................................

2. In bar 4 of the right hand of the piano part, indicated by the asterisk, add a rest to complete the bar.

3. In bar 1 of the piano part, add a dynamic marking to indicate that the pianist should play loudly.

4. In bar 4 of the drum part, add the following notes:

   Beat 1:   Two eighth-note bass drums

   Beat 2:   Two eighth-note snare drums

   Beat 3:   An eighth-note rest followed by an eighth-note bass drum

   Beat 4:   An eighth-note rest followed by an eighth-note snare

5. In bar 1 of the bass-guitar part, add a musical symbol between beats 3 and 4 to indicate that the bassist should play a slide between the notes.

6. Which part plays the same rhythm in all four bars? *(Tick one box)*

   ☐ Piano (right hand)

   ☐ Piano (left hand)

   ☐ Bass guitar

   ☐ Drums

7. Add a staccato symbol to the lowest note in the right hand of the piano part.

8. Name the two drum voices that play on beat 1 of bar 2:

   *Your answer:* ......................................................................................................................................

9. In bar 1 of the bass-guitar part, which note is not part of the named chord?

   *Your answer:* ......................................................................................................................................

10. How many times is the crash cymbal played in bars 1 to 4 of the drum part?

    *Your answer:* ......................................................................................................................................

11. Name the melodic interval formed between the first two notes of bar 3 of the right hand of the piano part:

    *Your answer:* ......................................................................................................................................

12. Name the note with an accidental in bar 2 of the bass-guitar part:

    *Your answer:* ......................................................................................................................................

# Section 4 | Band Analysis

13. Which part contains the longest note of the piece? *(Tick one box)*

    ☐ Piano (right hand)

    ☐ Piano (left hand)

    ☐ Bass guitar

    ☐ Drums

14. Add a musical symbol to the final bar of the piano part to show that it increases in volume throughout.

15. Which part does not have a key signature?

    *Your answer:* .................................................................................................................................................

# SAMPLE PAPER

The following pages contain examples of the types of questions you will find in a Grade 1 exam paper. They give an indication of the content, format, layout and level at this grade.

You will see the exam paper has been split into the same four sections that have been presented earlier in this workbook:

- Music Notation
- Popular Music Harmony
- Band Knowledge
- Band Analysis

## Content Overview

- **Marking:**
  - The exam is marked out of a total of 100, and the total available marks for each section are clearly stated at the start of each section. There is also a blank markbox where your total examination score can be noted.
  - The total marks available for each question are displayed on the right, and include a space for your teacher to mark your answers.

- **General advice:**
  - If a question requires a written answer, don't feel compelled to use every line. Answering the question correctly is much more important than using all the available space.
  - Aim to answer all the questions set. If you get stuck on one particular question, move on and come back to it later.

- **Neatness:**
  - Your answers should be neat, accurate and legible as marks cannot be given if your response is ambiguous.
  - Avoid unnecessary corrections by thinking your responses through before committing them to paper.
  - Use a pencil that is sharp enough to write precisely, but soft enough to rub out and make corrections.
  - To avoid confusion, tick boxes (checkboxes) should be marked with a clear tick symbol rather than a cross. Please note that some answers require more than one box to be ticked, so read the questions carefully.

Please visit *www.rockschool.co.uk* for detailed information on all Rockschool examinations, including syllabus guides, marking schemes and examination entry information.

# Grade 1 | Sample Paper

**Section 1 | Music Notation**

Mark:

**Q 1.01 | Identify the missing time signature:** *(Tick one box)*

1

☐ 2/4     ☐ 3/4     ☐ 4/4

-----------------------------------------------------------------------

**Q 1.02 | Identify the missing time signature:** *(Tick one box)*

1

☐ 2/4     ☐ 3/4     ☐ 4/4

-----------------------------------------------------------------------

**Q 1.03 | Identify the missing note as indicated with a question mark:** *(Tick one box)*

1

☐ ♩     ☐ ♪     ☐ 𝅗𝅥

-----------------------------------------------------------------------

**Q 1.04 | Identify the missing rest as indicated with a question mark:** *(Tick one box)*

1

☐ 𝄽     ☐ 𝄾     ☐ 𝄽.

-----------------------------------------------------------------------

**Q 1.05** | Add the three note and rest values together and identify the matching note value: *(Tick one box)*  [ 1 ]

☐ ♩  ☐ ♩.  ☐ ♩

---

**Q 1.06** | Add the three note values together and identify the matching note value: *(Tick one box)*  [ 1 ]

☐ ♩.  ☐ ♩.  ☐ 𝅝

---

**Q 1.07** | Which note has the same value as the written rest? *(Tick one box)*  [ 1 ]

☐ ♩.  ☐ ♪.  ☐ ♩.

---

**Q 1.08** | Which rest has the same value as the written note? *(Tick one box)*  [ 1 ]

☐ 𝄽.  ☐ 𝄾.  ☐ ▬.

---

**Q 1.09** | The following scale is F major. Add the missing clef:  [ 1 ]

**Q 1.10** | The following scale is G major. Add the missing clef:

**Q 1.11** | How does a dot placed to the right of a notehead affect the note? *(Tick one box)*

☐ It makes the note longer.

☐ It makes the note shorter.

☐ It makes the note louder.

**Q 1.12** | Which is the musical term for the following symbol? *(Tick one box)*

☐ Decrescendo      ☐ Legato      ☐ Crescendo

**Q 1.13** | What is the meaning of the following musical symbol? *(Tick one box)*

*p*

☐ Play quietly      ☐ Play loudly      ☐ Play smoothly

**Q 1.14** | Which is the correct musical notation for the musical term 'staccato'? *(Tick one box)*

**Q 1.15** | Which is the correct symbol for the musical term 'decrescendo'? *(Tick one box)*   `1`

☐ *f*

☐ >

☐ —

---

**Q 1.16** | Circle the three consecutive notes that form the F major chord in the stave below:   `3`

---

**Q 1.17** | Add a note of the correct length above each question mark so that each bar matches the time signature:   `2`

---

## Section 2 | Popular Music Harmony

**Total marks for this section:** `25`

**Mark:**

**Q 2.01** | Write 'S' in the boxes between notes that are a Semitone apart:   `2`

# Grade 1 | Sample Paper

**Q 2.02 |** Add a note to the right of each of the notes to create the requested melodic interval:  `[3]`

major 2nd                                   major 3rd                                   major 3rd

---

**Q 2.03 |** Using whole notes, write a one-octave *ascending* scale of G major. Use accidentals instead of a key signature:  `[5]`

---

**Q 2.04 |** Using whole notes, write a one-octave *descending* scale of F major. Use accidentals instead of a key signature:  `[5]`

---

**Q 2.05 |** Using whole notes, write a one-octave *ascending* arpeggio in the major key shown by the key signature below:  `[5]`

---

**Q 2.06 |** Circle the group of three notes that form a G chord:  `[1]`

G B C          G A D          G B D          G F A          G C E

---

**Q 2.07 |** Circle the group of three notes that form a C chord:  `[1]`

C D E          C E G          C G B          C E F          C F A

---

**Q 2.08** | Circle the group of three notes that form an F chord:

1

F G A       F E G       F G B       F A E       F A C

---

**Q 2.09** | Circle the major chord that shares its name with the key indicated by the key signature and clef. Finally, add the chord name on the line below the stave:

2

*Your answer:*

---

**Section 3 | Band Knowledge | Part 1 – Identification**

Total marks for this section: 25

Mark:

*The following three questions refer to the labelled image of a drum kit on the right:*

**Q 3.01** | Which letter corresponds to the ride cymbal? *(Tick one box)*

1

☐ A   ☐ B   ☐ C   ☐ D   ☐ E

**Q 3.02** | Which letter corresponds to the crash cymbal? *(Tick one box)*

1

☐ A   ☐ B   ☐ C   ☐ D   ☐ E

**Q 3.03** | Which letter corresponds to the hi-hat? *(Tick one box)*

1

☐ A   ☐ B   ☐ C   ☐ D   ☐ E

# Grade 1 | Sample Paper

The following three questions refer to the labelled image below:

**Q 3.04** | What is the correct name for the part of the instrument labelled 'A'? *(Tick one box)* [1]

☐ Foot    ☐ Arm    ☐ Body    ☐ Neck

**Q 3.05** | What is the correct name for the part of the instrument labelled 'B'? *(Tick one box)* [1]

☐ Foot    ☐ Arm    ☐ Body    ☐ Neck

**Q 3.06** | What type of instrument is shown in the image? [1]

*Your answer:* .................................................................................................................................

---

**Q 3.07** | Identify the correct statement below: *(Tick one box)* [1]

☐ A bass guitar has more strings than an electric guitar.

☐ A bass guitar has fewer strings than an electric guitar.

☐ A bass guitar has the same number of strings as an electric guitar.

---

**Q 3.08** | An electronic keyboard is often supplied with an external box wired with a plug. This is used to supply the correct amount of electrical current to the keyboard. What is it called? *(Tick one box)* [1]

☐ Power adaptor    ☐ Fuse box    ☐ Battery case    ☐ Synthesiser

---

**Q 3.09** | Identify the correct statement below: *(Tick one box)* ☐ 1

☐ There is the same number of white keys and blacks keys on a piano keyboard.

☐ There are more black keys than white keys on a piano keyboard.

☐ There are more white keys than black keys on a piano keyboard.

---

**Q 3.10** | One of the white keys, found approximately in the centre of the keyboard, is commonly used as a reference point on the keyboard. What is this note called? *(Tick one box)* ☐ 1

☐ Top C          ☐ Middle C          ☐ Key of C          ☐ CV

---

**Q 3.11** | Which part of the body has control muscles that allow a singer to change the shape and space of their oral cavity, allowing them to form different sounds? *(Tick one box)* ☐ 1

☐ Trachea     ☐ Jaw     ☐ Lungs     ☐ Mouth

---

**Q 3.12** | What tube allows air to pass through the oral cavity and into the organs with which you breathe? *(Tick one box)* ☐ 1

☐ Trachea     ☐ Jaw     ☐ Lungs     ☐ Mouth

---

**Q 3.13** | Which major organ allows you to breathe as well as sing? *(Tick one box)* ☐ 1

☐ Trachea     ☐ Jaw     ☐ Lungs     ☐ Mouth

## Section 3 | Band Knowledge | Part 2 – Notation & Techniques

The following three questions relate to the one-bar extract of drum notation on the right:

**Q 3.14** | Which drum voice plays with the bass drum on the first beat of the bar? *(Tick one box)* [ 1 ]

☐ Hi-hat     ☐ Snare     ☐ Crash     ☐ Ride

**Q 3.15** | What does the circle over the third beat of the bar indicate? *(Tick one box)* [ 1 ]

☐ Open hi-hat     ☐ Closed hi-hat     ☐ Accented crash

**Q 3.16** | Do the stems for the cymbals go up or down? *(Tick one box)* [ 1 ]

☐ Up     ☐ Down     ☐ Both directions

---

The following three questions relate to the one-bar extract of guitar notation on the right:

**Q 3.17** | Name the technique used on beats 1 & 2, indicated by a 'slur' in the notation: [ 1 ]

*Your answer:* ....................................................................................

**Q 3.18** | Name the technique used on beat 3, indicated by a straight line in the notation: [ 1 ]

*Your answer:* ....................................................................................

**Q 3.19** | Describe how the articulation on the last note of the bar will affect the sound of the note: [ 1 ]

*Your answer:* ....................................................................................

*The following three questions relate to the one-bar extract of piano music on the right:*

**Q 3.20** | Which hand or hands play the melody? *(Tick one box)* | 1 |

☐ Left    ☐ Right    ☐ Both

**Q 3.21** | Which hand or hands play staccato throughout? *(Tick one box)* | 1 |

☐ Left    ☐ Right    ☐ Both

**Q 3.22** | What is the correct meaning of the term 'legato'? *(Tick one box)* | 1 |

☐ Play smoothly    ☐ Play slowly    ☐ Play loudly

---

*The following two tasks relate to the one-bar extract of vocal notation on the right:*

No - thing but the sea and sky

**Q 3.23** | Add a staccato articulation to the final note of the bar. | 1 |

**Q 3.24** | Add a portamento articulation between the first two notes of the bar. | 1 |

**Q 3.25** | What is the correct meaning of the term 'portamento'? *(Tick one box)* | 1 |

☐ Sing with a smooth pitch slide from the first to the second note.

☐ Sing the notes with a gradual increase in volume.

☐ The notes should be spoken rather than sung.

# Grade 1 | Sample Paper

## Section 4 | Band Analysis

Total marks for this section: 30

Mark:

*The following 12 questions relate to the four-bar score below. Note that bar 4 has blank areas to be filled in as part of the tasks below:*

**Q 4.01 |** Name the note in bar 1 of the guitar part that is not found in the chord written above the bar:  1

*Your answer:*

**Q 4.02 |** In the guitar part, add a symbol to indicate that the two eighth notes in bar 1 are played as a pull-off.  2

**Q 4.03 |** Which scale does the guitar use to play its melody?  1

*Your answer:*

**Q 4.04 |** In the bass part, add a slide symbol between the last note of bar 3 and the first note of bar 4.  2

**Q 4.05 |** In the bass part, add the missing rest after the final note in bar 4.  2

**Q 4.06** | How many eighth notes would give the equivalent note value to the dotted note played by the bass in bar 2? *(Tick one box)*  $\boxed{2}$

☐ 1   ☐ 2   ☐ 3   ☐ 4   ☐ 5   ☐ 6

**Q 4.07** | In the drum part, add a crescendo marking in bar 4 under beats 1 and 2, then a decrescendo under beats 3 and 4.  $\boxed{4}$

**Q 4.08** | Add an open hi-hat indication to the first note of bar 2 and a closed hi-hat indication to the second note of bar 2.  $\boxed{4}$

**Q 4.09** | Which is the correct statement? *(Tick one box)*  $\boxed{2}$

☐ The ride cymbal is played in bars 1 & 3.

☐ The ride cymbal is only played in bar 1.

☐ The ride cymbal is not played at all.

☐ The ride cymbal is played in all four bars.

**Q 4.10** | What are the two drum voices that play on the first note of bar 1? *(Tick two boxes)*  $\boxed{2}$

☐ Bass drum

☐ Snare drum

☐ Hi-hat

☐ Crash cymbal

☐ Ride cymbal

**Q 4.11** | Add a hi-hat part to bar 4 in the following rhythm:  $\boxed{6}$

*Two quarter notes followed by four eighth notes.*

**Q 4.12** | In which bar does the bass guitar play the same rhythm as the bass drum and snare drum? *(Tick one box)*  $\boxed{2}$

☐ Bar 1

☐ Bar 2

☐ Bar 3

☐ Bar 4

## Syllabus Content Overview | Grade 1

**Important:** This table represents content that is new at this grade. The content of Rockschool Theory Examinations is cumulative, so Grades 1 to 8 include all content from previous grades in the syllabus. A full version of this table is available online at *www.rockschool.co.uk*, and includes details of content at every grade.

| Section | Content | Details |
|---|---|---|
| **1: Music Notation (20%)** | 1.1: Pitch | note range: bass clef (D2–D4), treble clef (B3–B5) |
| | 1.2: Note length/rhythm | note lengths: dotted whole, dotted half, dotted quarter, dotted eighth notes, equivalent rests |
| | | tied notes |
| | 1.3: Dynamics, articulations, phrasing | dynamics: piano, forte, crescendo (cresc.), diminuendo (dim.) |
| | | articulations: staccato, legato, accents |
| **2: Popular Music Harmony (25%)** | 2.1: Major scales and related intervals | major scale: F |
| | | harmonic and melodic intervals: major 2nd, major 3rd |
| | 2.2: Simple triadic chords | major arpeggios: F |
| | | major chord formula |
| | | major chords: C, G, F |
| **3: Band Knowledge (25%)** | 3.1: Identify instrument parts and function | drums: ride cymbal, crash cymbal |
| | | guitar and bass guitar: body, neck |
| | | keys: middle C, adaptor socket, power button |
| | | vocals: jaw, trachea |
| | 3.2: Identify instrument-specific notation | drum notation: ride cymbal, crash cymbal, open hi-hat, closed hi-hat |
| | | guitar and bass-guitar notation: staccato, pull-offs, slides |
| | | keys notation: legato, staccato |
| | | vocal notation: portamento |
| | 3.3: Identify instrumental techniques | as listed above in 3.2 |
| **4: Band Analysis (30%)** | 4.1: Identify general music features listed within criteria 1, 2 and 3 within a score | identify and show understanding of the applied musical elements listed within the first three sections (above) within the context of a score |
| | | instrument range: drums (hi-hat, snare drum, bass drum, crash cymbal, ride cymbal), guitar, bass guitar, keyboard, vocals |
| | | number of parts: 3 |
| | | piece length: 4 bars |
| | 4.2: Accurately complete a score | 1 bar, within any part: rhythm, pitch, chord names, articulations, dynamics, tempo |
| | 4.3: Identify instrument-specific techniques | as listed within part 3 (above) |

# rockschool®

# ENTER ONLINE

## Ready to take your Rockschool Theory Exam?

## Now it's easier than ever...

**1 GO TO WWW.ROCKSCHOOL.CO.UK/ENTER-ONLINE**

**2 CREATE AN ACCOUNT**

**3 SELECT YOUR EXAM CENTRE AND DATE**

**4 CHOOSE YOUR GRADE**

## ... and you're ready to go.

Book your exam today – go to **www.rockschool.co.uk/enter-online**, or email **info@rockschool.co.uk** for more information.